Winter Florals
Coloring Book

An Adult Coloring Book Featuring Winter Floral
Arrangements, Beautiful Holiday Bouquets
and Exquisite Christmas Flowers

an Imprint of **The Fruitful Mind Publishing LTD.**
www.coloringbookcafe.com

Have questions? Let us know.
support@coloringbookcafe.com

 facebook.com/coloringbookcafe  @coloringbookcafe

This Book
Belongs To:

Pine tree branches,
holly and Poinsettia

Desiccates epiphyllum

Mistletoe

Roses, holly, and dried lotus

Đried lotus, pine cone
and branches, poinsettia,
holly berries

Holly berries, amaryllis

Lemon branches

Succulents, tillandsia,

echeverias

Proteas flowers, dried branches, holly berries

Thistle, dog-rose berries, eucalyptus

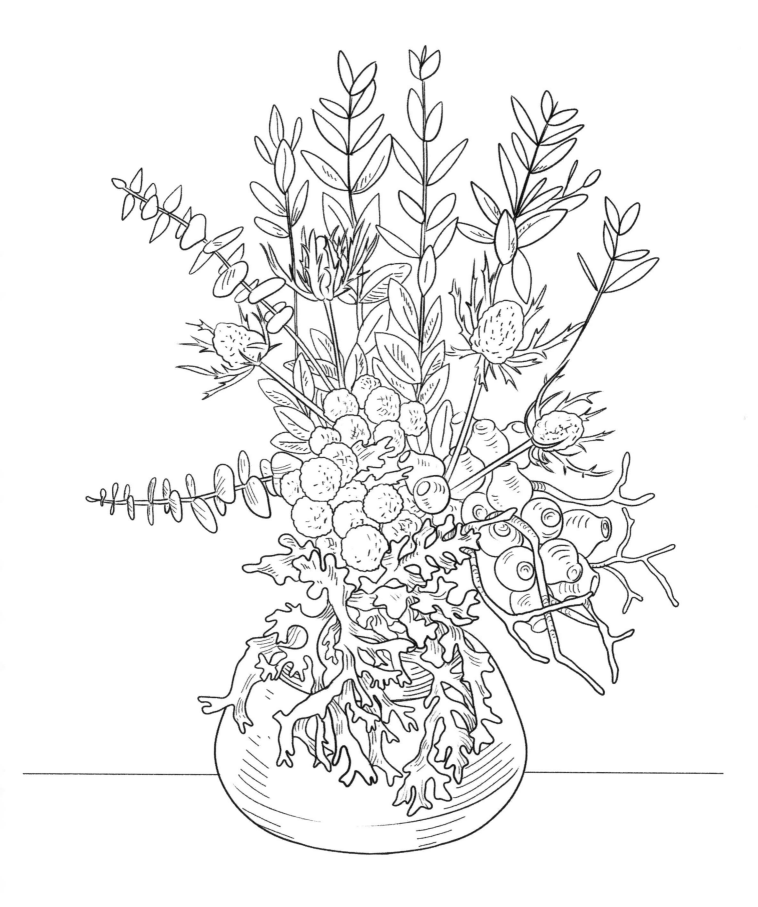

Carnations

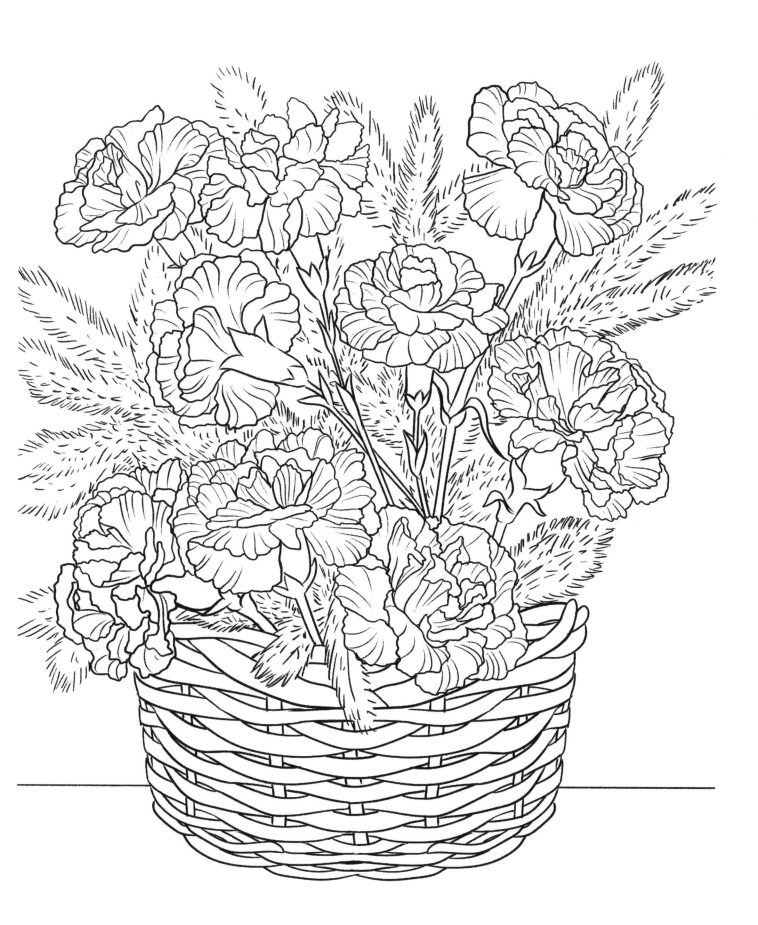

Baby orange tree

Gerbera

Thistle

Poinsettia

Chrysanthemum

Dog-rose berries, eucalyptus

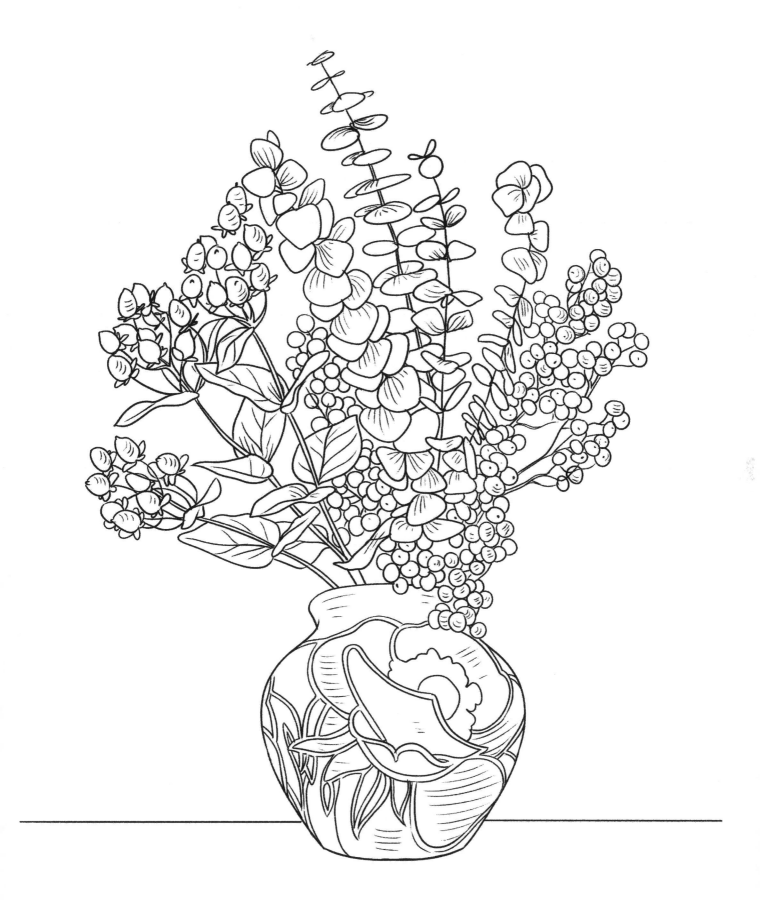

Dried lotus,
Chinese lantern plant

Proteas flowers, eucalyptus,
dried poppy

Dog rose

Anemones

Hellebore

Pine, dried lotus, dried poppy, holly berries, dried oranges

Dried oranges, pine branches, pine cones, dog rose berries

Succulents, fake decorative flowers, holly berries, pine branches

Made in the USA
Columbia, SC
04 December 2019